IMAGES
of England

HANDSWORTH,
HOCKLEY AND
HANDSWORTH WOOD

A view of Handsworth old church taken from across Victoria Park.

IMAGES
of England

HANDSWORTH, HOCKLEY AND HANDSWORTH WOOD

Compiled by
Peter Drake

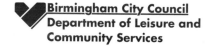

Birmingham City Council
Department of Leisure and
Community Services

TEMPUS

First published 1998, reprinted 2001
Copyright © Peter Drake, 1998

Tempus Publishing Limited
The Mill, Brimscombe Port,
Stroud, Gloucestershire, GL5 2QG

ISBN 0 7524 1551 4

Typesetting and origination by
Tempus Publishing Limited
Printed in Great Britain by
Midway Clark Printing, Wiltshire

A rural scene in Handsworth in the 1860s. This picture was reproduced from the painting by
John Joseph Hughes, the Birmingham landscape painter.

Contents

A procession in Soho Road in the early years of this century.

Introduction

Handsworth is one of Birmingham's best known suburbs and a range of associations spring to mind when Handsworth is mentioned. In recent years the Handsworth Carnival, that joyous street celebration of the city's and the suburb's West Indian culture, has attracted huge crowds. Before that Handsworth Park was for many years the venue for flower shows, dog shows, scout rallies and other events which attracted a national following to the park. Less felicitously, the Handsworth Riots of 1985 focused nationwide attention on one small area of Handsworth, the Lozells Road. What probably does not immediately spring to mind when Handsworth is mentioned is its important historical associations, and yet Handsworth was the home of Matthew Boulton's and James Watt's Soho Manufactory, probably the most inventive and famous manufactory in the world in the late eighteenth and early nineteenth centuries.

Handsworth spreads north west from the city and the photographs reproduced here cover a wide area from almost inner city Hockley down the Soho Road, the heart of Handsworth, and out to the adjacent but far leafier and residential Handsworth Wood. Although Handsworth had its own local authority status, separate from Birmingham up to 1911, and indeed its old town hall still remains, there never has been a real High Street or village centre. Rather, the Soho Road has acted as both the main shopping street and the main road north west out of Birmingham to West Bromwich.

The geography of Handsworth today reflects the piecemeal development of the area. At the beginning of the nineteenth century Handsworth amounted to little more than a small group of hamlets with some residual agriculture and a population just touching the 2,000 mark. Even in the 1860s the *Staffordshire Directory* described the parish as 'extending over 8,000 acres and forming a fashionable suburb to the north west of Birmingham, and containing many handsome mansions and villa residences of the businessmen of Birmingham.' The population at the 1861 census was 11,000. By this date the contrasts between Hockley and Handsworth on the one hand and Handsworth Wood on the other were becoming clearer. House building in Handsworth and Hockley, particularly in the late nineteenth century, was rapid and unplanned. By the end of the century Handsworth was a fully developed late Victorian suburb with a varied assortment of housing styles mixed in with small industrial undertakings. As the city spread outwards to house its workforce, many of whom worked in the neighbouring jewellery quarter, so more land was built over and the Handsworth of today took shape. This process of urbanization is most graphically illustrated in the rise and decline of the Soho Manufactory. Brought to the area initially by the presence of waterpower in the Hockley valley and because, despite its proximity to Birmingham, the land was undeveloped, the manufactory became a worldwide phenomenon only to be demolished and replaced by housing in the 1860s.

Handsworth Wood, though, was further from the city and was largely immune to these developments. Indeed this is a description of the area in 1931 taken from an estate agent's brochure: 'Within about four miles of the centre of Birmingham there lies a pleasant stretch of open country – undulating and well wooded, rich in glorious views, dotted with stately country mansions of the Georgian time and with famous old farmsteads around which the cattle graze unconcernedly ... a quiet, restful and conspicuously healthy environment in which to make ones home'. This brochure was advertising semi-detached homes without garages for £380 while grand family houses were being sold for £1,500. Handsworth Wood is still regarded today as one of Birmingham's best residential areas with house prices at a slightly higher level.

In March 1978 an elderly ex-resident of Handsworth wrote to the *Birmingham Post* describing his youth in the suburb 'I lived in Handsworth from the age of four until I was sixteen. It is for my friends to say if it harmed me, but I am not aware that it was other than as happy a time as one can expect from youth. If you ask what there was for the young to do it is hard to answer. I remember a halfpenny tram ride that eventually got us to Sutton Park, walks to Barr Beacon, damming the stream at Great Barr on the way, tennis in Handsworth Park, visits to Grove Lane Baths, cycling round the square and football on the playing field in Rookery Road. For summer holidays we cycled to North Wales'. Hopefully this collection of photographs will evoke similar nostalgic memories of this fascinating district.

The photographs reproduced here, nearly all for the first time, reflect the contrasts between different areas. The images of the gypsies on the Black Patch in Hockley (see p. 71-5) are a world away from the life led by the owner of the splendid mansions of Hansworth and Handsworth Wood. All of the photographs have been copied from the extensive collections in the Local Studies section of Birmingham Central Library.

Further information on Handsworth's history, as well as many more photographs, can be found there as well as through the Handsworth Historical Society which has regular open days at the old town hall.

One
Rural Scenes

The Shell Pool near to South Road. The pool was part of Soho Park in the grounds of what had been the Soho Manufactory.

Warstone Pool near Forge Lane on the Sandwell Park boundary of Handsworth, 1899. It often appears on maps as Swan Pool.

A cornfield with Asbury Wesleyan chapel spire in the distance. The view was taken from the junction of Rookery and Albert Roads, 1898.

The view in Oxhill Road looking towards Sandwell Road.

The same road, with a different name. Stockwell Lane (above), as it was called then, but Friary Road (below) as it is called now, looking north east with an old farmhouse on the right of the top photograph.

Sycamore Farm photographed from Queens Head Road.

Sycamore House and Farm, 1902. Sycamore House was built for William Murdock. (There are further views of the house on p. 32).

An old farm on the site of what became the Rookery Road schools.

Bradley's Farm on Rookery Road, 1906.

Lea Hall Farm, Wood Lane.

Old houses in College Road, 1897. This picture was photographed by C.L. Stait or the Warwickshire Photographic Survey.

Another posed view, taken at Shell Pool and showing 1890s fashion. The pool was soon to be filled in and houses built on it on the north side of South Road. Early ordinance survey maps clearly show the shell-like shape of the pool and hence its name.

Two
Soho

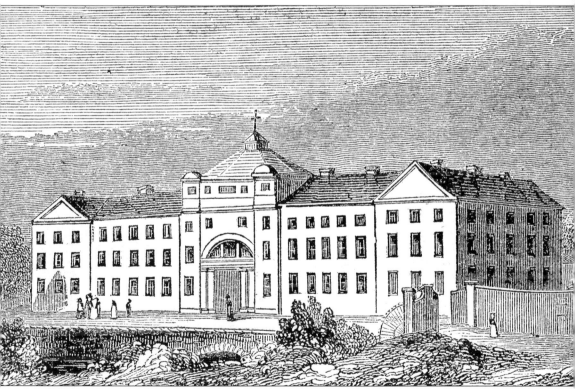

Soho Manufactory. The largest factory in the world, it opened at the then huge cost of £10,000 in 1762 and was the brainchild of Matthew Boulton, the Birmingham born and bred industrialist. Outgrowing his original premises in Birmingham town centre, he conceived and built the new factory on what was then the uninhabited heartland of Soho, less than two miles from the old works. He utilized the water power of Hockey Brook.

This is how the manufactory was described in the *Birmingham Directory* of 1774: 'Four Squares with shops, warehouses etc for a thousand workmen who, in a great variety of Branches, excel in their several departments; not only in the fabrications of Buttons, Boxes, Trinkets etc, in Gold and Silver, but in many other Arts, long predominant in France, which lose their reputation on a comparison with the product of this place.'

A photograph taken around 1851, shortly before the demolition of the manufactory. It was reproduced from a wet collodion negative

The entrepreneurial nature of Boulton's enterprise at Soho is illustrated by the number of firms he took over. From making toys, trinkets and silver plate, the works expanded adding a coining mill in 1788, which produced 40,000 coins an hour, and in 1796 the Soho Foundry opened using James Watt's successful steam engine to make heavy metal goods.

Another view of the manufactory from a collection of four photographs acquired by Sir Benjamin Stone and added to his collection. The grounds were extensive and Boulton was applauded for turning 'a barren heath into a delightful garden'.

The manufactory being demolished in the 1860s, shortly after the death of James Watts Jnr, the son of Boulton's partner. Only a row of workmen's cottages, called Foundry Row, remain of the whole massive enterprise.

A view of the original grounds of the manufactory in 1899. This is the site of the Soho Mint on what became the east side of South Road.

Another view of the grounds. The archaeological series *Time Team* on Channel 4 made a programme about the site and a video of it is available to watch in Birmingham Central Library. It is salutary how comprehensively all traces of the original site have disappeared under bricks and tarmac.

Soho Foundry. A portion of the underground passage was still in use when this photograph was taken in 1941.

Soho Pool in 1868. It was constructed in 1759, for the firm of Ruston and Eaves and was taken over by Boulton. Later, it was turned into a pleasure resort named, after its proprietor, Knibbs Pool. The *Staffordshire Directory*, of 1868, described it as 'a beautiful sheet of water of 20 acres, situated amidst wooded and fine undulating scenery, the place of great resort during the summer months to the lovers of rowing.' The pool was filled in soon after this picture was taken.

Matthew Boulton was a well known industrialist and in some ways Birmingham's most famous son. The description 'industrialist' does not due justice to his many activities and interests; he was part entrepreneur, part venture capitalist, part craftsman, part inventor, part factory manager and he also had astonishing partnerships with James Watt and William Murdock which helped to develop the steam engine and gas lighting.

A view of Soho House taken by another famous Birmingham man, Sir Benjamin Stone, in 1883. The house, built by Boulton, looked down from the top of Soho Hill on to the manufactory and its grounds. Due to Boulton's reputation, it became a meeting place for the Lunar Society a group of industrialists, inventors, free thinkers and physicians who met there monthly 'on the night of the full moon.'

Soho House when it was used as a girls' boarding school in the 1890s. The house was used to being busy: in Boulton's days it seemed less like a home than 'an inn for the entertainment of strangers.'

Mrs Taylor, the head teacher, and some of her pupils in 1893. The property was subsequently used as a lodging house for single policemen. It has now being restored to its eighteenth-century appearance and was reopened by Birmingham City Council as a museum with an attractive visitor centre.

The drawing room at Soho House in 1906. In Boulton's day the house welcomed a staggering number of visitors from around the world who visited the famous manufactory and enjoyed the elegance and hospitality of Boulton in his White House. Among its visitors were the Empress Catherine of Russia, Lord Nelson and Lady Hamilton.

James Watt. The outstanding engineer of the first phase of the Industrial Revolution, he was responsible for the transformation of Soho Works through his invention of the steam engine. Originally from Scotland, he came to Birmingham in 1774 and died there in 1819.

Artistic representations of Watt's first and later inventions, doubtless based more on fancy than reality.

Heathfield, James Watt's house, photographed in 1901 when it was occupied by George Tangye. The house, built on what was then heathland, was designed by Samuel Wyatt and erected between 1787 and 1790. The house was demolished in 1928 to make way for the Heathfield estate.

A distant view of Heathfield taken from St Mary's churchyard in 1908. Like Boulton at Soho House, Watt created at Heathfield a small country estate for his retirement.

An exterior view of Watt's house showing the lightning conductor he erected which used flint clippings as a non-conductor.

James Watt's workrooms at Heathfield which were sealed in 1819, at the time of his death, and lay undisturbed until they were reopened and these photographs were taken in 1901. Subsequently the contents were removed to the Science Museum in South Kensington.

William Murdock, the third of the great figures indelibly linked with Handsworth. Like Watt, he left Scotland for Birmingham and is best remembered for his invention of gas lighting. The most wonderful demonstration of this involved the lighting of the Soho Manufactory to celebrate the Peace of Amiens in 1802.

Sycamore Hill House, the home of William Murdock. It was described in *Birmingham Faces and Places* as 'a conspicuous object from the Great Western Railway, halfway between Soho and Handsworth stations ... and may be approached from the village of Handsworth down the Queens Head Lane.'

A view of the house when it was being used as a children's home in 1904. The house, which bore many examples of Murdock's experiments, was subsequently demolished.

Three
Religious Connections

A postcard view of Handsworth parish church, St Mary's. The ancient parish of Handsworth covered a large area from the West Bromwich boundary to Lozells in one direction and from Hockey Brook to Sutton in the other. St Mary's was the only church that was built in the parish between Norman times and 1833.

An illustration of St Mary's by W. Collingwood. St Mary's was dubbed 'the Westminster Abbey of the Industrial Revolution' because it is the last resting place of Boulton, Watt and Murdock.

A view of the church in 1877.

16029 HANDSWORTH CHURCH.   BIRMINGHAM.

Another postcard view of the church, this time taken from across the tennis courts in Handsworth Park.

Interior of
Handsworth
Parish Church

The interior of the church. The writer of the postcard, in 1906, has marked with a cross her regular pew. There are busts and statues of Boulton, Watt and Murdock in the church.

St Michael's church off Soho Hill. The church was designed by William Bourne of Dudley and consecrated as a chapel of ease to St Mary's in 1855.

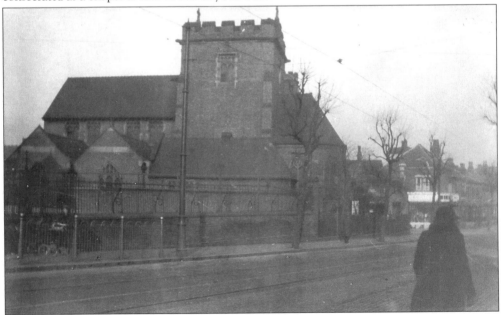

St Peter's church, a brick building in the Gothic style in Grove Lane, 1907.

St James' church, situated at the corner of Crocketts Road and St James Road. It was built between 1838 and 1840 as Handsworth began to expand.

St Andrew's church in Oxhill Road opened on 30 January 1909, with seats for 700 worshippers.

Somerset Road Wesleyan chapel, built in 1894. The photograph was taken by Thomas Lewis.

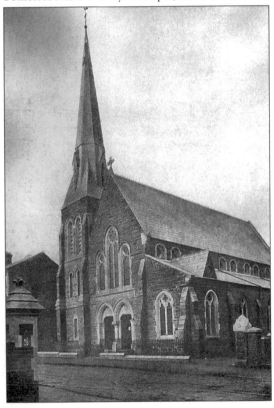

Wretham Road (Swedenborgian) church. The church was opened on 22 November 1876.

Union Row chapel in 1870. It was built in 1789 as a Wesleyan chapel, although it later became a Congregational church. The building became the first Gurdwara (Sikh Temple) in Handsworth in 1972 and has since been developed as a community project.

Soho Hill Congregational chapel. Built in 1892, it was well known as the home of the Soho Hill Men's Movement which played an important role in the district's religious life.

Bishop Latimer's Memorial church, a Grade II listed building. The church was designed by the well known architect W.H. Bidlake and built between 1903 and 1904. It is described in the listing citation as 'A very large church akin to an East Anglian Perpendicular wool church.'

Handsworth Rectory, 1892. This house, with its considerable grounds, occupied approximately, the site where the Victoria Park pool now is.

Handsworth Rectory. This photograph comes from the Sir Benjamin Stone Collection, one of the Central Library's finest collections of Victorian photographs.

St George's Rectory, Hockey Hill, 1901.

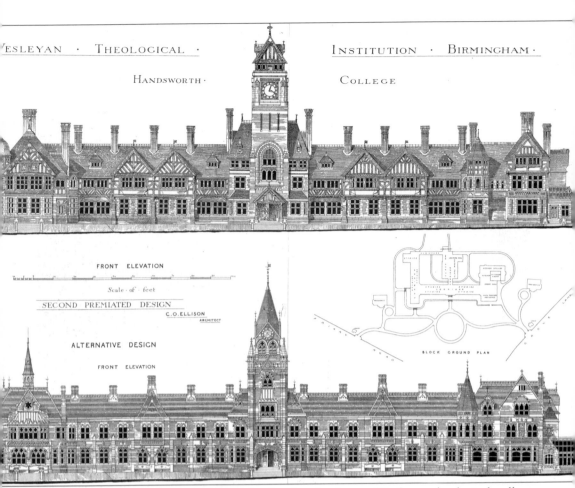

WESLEYAN · THEOLOGICAL · INSTITUTION · BIRMINGHAM ·

HANDSWORTH · **COLLEGE**

FRONT ELEVATION

Scale · of · feet

SECOND PREMIATED DESIGN

C.O.ELLISON
ARCHITECT

ALTERNATIVE DESIGN

FRONT ELEVATION

BLOCK GROUND PLAN

One of Handsworth's most prominent landmarks, the former Wesleyan theological college which is now a Grade II listed building. These plans appeared in *Building News* in July 1879. The college opened the following year with fifty-four students in residence under the principal, the Revd Henry Bett.

The college, photographed from the bottom of Friary Road. Handsworth was chosen as the site of the college partly because its location between Birmingham and the Black Country contained a group of circuits where the students would be able to exercise their preaching gifts to good effect.

A postcard view. In 1970 the college joined Queens College to provide more ecumenical theological training and it is now used as residences for students from Aston University.

The College entrance. The building has Grade II listed status.

A close up of the doorway, 1898. The building is in the Gothic style of the fourteenth century.

Four
Splendid Mansions

Waverhill House, Soho Road, around 1875. This was the home of John Rhodes, a local philanthropist, who left money to build the Rhodes Almshouses also on the Soho Road.

Hockley Abbey in 1868. The name is a misnomer because the house had no religious connections at all. It was built around 1770 by a local manufacturer on a site at the head of Soho Pool.

The house was locally it was known as Cinder House but, as its style resembled a monastery, it was also dubbed Hockley Abbey. These photographs show it in a derelict state after it fell into disuse after 1860.

Thornhill House. Built in 1826 for Matthew Boulton's daughter, the house was demolished in 1900.

This photograph shows a visit to the house from Mr Vale a local fruiterer, around 1890.

The entrance to Thornhill House, off Soho Road, on the left. The house was situated almost opposite the library. The Rope Walk was in the grounds.

The lodge to Thornhill House with Mr Dale in the doorway.

Another fine Handsworth residence, Cavendish House, photographed in 1880.

The Austin's house, in 1931, shortly before its demolition. Described in the estate agent's brochure as being 'charmingly situated in its own grounds with lake, wood land and dell', it was built by John Whateley, a wealthy gentleman farmer, in the eighteenth century.

The Austins, photographed from Landgate Road. The house occupied a high position with splendid views to West Bromwich. The present Austin Road, linking Holyhead Road and Island Road, approximately occupies the site of the carriageway to the house.

The premises of W. Lock and Company, jewellery manufacturers, at No. 141 Hockley Hill in 1901. Hockley Hill is on the fringes of Birmingham's main jewellery quarter.

The Limes on Soho Road, 1903. The house was near to Linwood Road and was demolished to make way for new shops.

A rear view of the friary in 1937. It was a Regency type house, built in 1658, which stood well back from Friary Road with a four acre paddock in front.

Endwood Court when it was the residence of J.B. Clarke JP. It was built for the industrialist James Russell of Wednesbury in the Gothic style in 1839. It was much altered and reduced in the 1930s and replaced by flats in the 1960s.

Five

Public Buildings and Schools

Handsworth's public offices and free library. This was the front cover of the *Handsworth Illustrated Local Chronicle* in 1880.

Two views of the Cruck House or Handsworth Old Town Hall in 1936.

The house was probably built in the early sixteenth century and divided into cottages and a hall in the early seventeenth century. It is one of the best examples of the early cruck timber construction in the country and is now a listed building. It was modernized in 1947 to form two dwellings and one part is now periodically used by the Handsworth Historical Society for open days and with displays of local photographs, newspapers and maps.

The old parish offices in Baker Street in 1908. This small, unimposing building was erected in 1830 and served as the parish offices for several years. It was later used as a warehouse before eventually being demolished in 1961.

The original police station in Handsworth in 1880. It was situated on Holyhead Road opposite Farcroft Avenue. In 1938 a new station was opened next door to the original one.

Another reminder of Handsworth's rural past, the Handsworth Pound in 1908. The pound was situated near to St Mary's church in Hamstead Road, was used to house stray animals.

Isaac George, the keeper of the pound, 1908. George, a blacksmith who lived opposite the pound, was paid £5 yearly and allowed to charge owners of stray horses for the cost of fodder.

An early view of Handsworth council house and library. The offices of the Handsworth UDC were erected in 1878-9 on the site of the Waggon and Horses Inn. The total cost of building and furnishings was £14,000.

The council house in a postcard view. The library first opened its doors on 1 May 1880.

A slightly busier
Soho Road and
library in 1962.

The changing face of Handsworth Library. The top photograph shows the library in 1913, the bottom photograph shows the library seventy years later, still serving the residents of Handsworth.

59

Handsworth Public Work Department's horse parade in 1911. The photograph was taken in the council house yard in front of the stables. Prizes were awarded by the department for the best horse and harness.

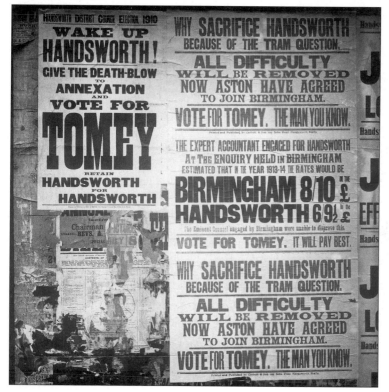

A reminder of the fight to keep Handsworth independent from the city of Birmingham. A poster from the losing anti-Birmingham candidate in the 1911 local elections, shortly after the Greater Birmingham Bill was passed and Handsworth was incorporated into Birmingham.

Handsworth fire brigade at its Birchfield Road station, around the turn of the century.

The brigade was founded in 1878, before which the local council had made no attempt to provide fire appliances for the area. The Birchfield branch fire station was opened in 1890.

Handsworth Cemetery entrance from the Holyhead Road. This was original entrance to the Leveretts, a large eighteenth-century house which occupied the cemetery site.

A postcard multi-view of Handsworth Cemetery.

The cemetery chapel in 1925.

The first burial at Handsworth Cemetery on 22 November 1909.

Grove Lane Baths. Handsworth UDC had purchased land at the corner of Grove Lane and Hinstock Road in 1901, as a site for the baths, and a local architect John Osborne designed the building. They were formally opened on 28 January 1907.

A view of the first class baths. It was described in the opening brochure as 'a pond measuring 100 ft by 35 ft, and is believed to be the finest swimming bath in the Midlands.' There were sixty dressing rooms.

MEMBERS OF THE BATHS AND PARKS COMMITTEE AND CHIEF OFFICERS.

COUNCILLOR HUMPHREYS — MR. H. RICHARDSON (SURVEYOR) — MR. E. WARD (DEPUTY CLERK) — COUNCILLOR NICKOLDS — COUNCILLOR BAINES — COUNCILLOR FEARN — MR. E. B. PINCKNEY (ACCOUNTANT CLERK)

COUNCILLOR FREELAND — COUNCILLOR SANDERS — COUNCILLOR LEMPRIERE — MR. H. WARD (CLERK) — COUNCILLOR EDWARDS (CHAIRMAN OF COUNCIL) — COUNCILLOR WHITE (CHAIRMAN OF COMMITTEE) — COUNCILLOR GRIFFITH — COUNCILLOR HOLDSWORTH (VICE-CHAIRMAN OF COUNCIL)

Members of Handsworth's bath's committee at the opening of the baths.

The main entrance to the baths, showing the separate entrances for men and women. The illustration is taken from the opening brochure. The baths have now closed and the building has been converted to residential use.

Handsworth Ladies College. The college, a preparatory school for young ladies, opened in 1872 at Milton House, Park Road. It offered a superior education at moderate fees. Apart from the basic curriculum, German, maths, harmony, piano and dancing were charged as extras. The school was highly successful academically and moved to larger premises. In 1891 it was situated at the corner of Hamstead Road and Villa Road and was reported to be for sale.

Building the new Handsworth girls' grammar school in 1910. The view shows Old Crick Lane which was closed after the making of Rose Hill Road.

Final touches by workmen before the school's opening in 1911.

The pupils were drawn from three existing King Edward's schools, at Aston, Surnmer Row and Bath Row.

Handsworth grammar school for boys. Formerly known as The Bridge Trust school, it opened on 5 August 1862 and consisted of one main room alongside two smaller classrooms and a board room. The original fifty-nine students were examined in reading, writing and arithmetic and selected by the headmaster, Revd James Merrick Guest. It became Handsworth grammar school in 1890.

The school from a 1960s postcard. It is still situated at its original Grove Lane site, focused around 'the big schoolroom' which is now used as the assembly hall.

Handsworth Wood boys' school, Church Lane. The school has just closed amidst some controversy. In recent years the school had become a comprehensive high school with a pupil intake reflecting the cultural diversity of the area.

Handsworth Wood girls' school, photographed at its opening in 1957. It opened with approximately 500 girls, most of them transferring from Grove Lane girls' Secondary Modern school, and a staff of sixteen including the headmistress, Miss Wheeler. The school is currently a culturally mixed comprehensive high school with over 600 girls on the roll.

Six

The Black Patch and the Rope Walk

A group of gypsies on the Black Patch, 1898.

A gypsy encampment on the Black Patch, 1898. This was an area of open ground between Winson Green and Handsworth which was used as dumping ground for slag from nearby furnaces.

Romanies colonized a part of the Black Patch between Hockley Brook and the railway line for their winter quarters having spent the summer travelling the Midlands.

The Romanies were a tightly knit group of families including the Smiths, Loveridges, Badgers, Claytons and Davises. The 'King' of this group was Esau Smith pictured here holding the horse on the right of the photograph. He was a well respected judge of a horse and his death, in 1901 aged 92, saw an elaborate burial at Handsworth old church. His wife, 'Queen Henty', is standing at the back of the photograph on the left. The 1891 census showed twenty-three families living on the encampment including thirty-three Smiths and twenty-eight Loveridges.

'Queen Henty.' Most of the gypsies were turned off the Black Patch in 1905, but 'Queen Henty' and a few others were allowed to stay until after her death in January 1907.

Hockley Brook in the foreground. The Romanies set up a gypsy chapel where they worshipped and, along with their caravans the site, had tents and huts as well as cultivated areas.

Black Patch Park, November 1981. After the gypsies were turned off the site, it was purchased by the Open Space Society for £10,000 and turned into a park with the intention of converting the Black Patch into a green one. It had to be enclosed with stout iron railing to prevent the gypsies retaking it.

The Rope Walk looking from Soho Road railway station in 1900. This was a very simple, if land hungry, way of manufacturing rope. The walk was owned by a firm called Haines.

The Rope Walk. The firm closed after the death of Mr Haines around 1914.

The Rope Walk was situated just outside the grounds of Thornhill House which can just be seen at the top of the photograph.

Another view of Thornhill House and the Rope Walk.

Seven

Pubs, Cinemas and the Park

The children's playground in Handsworth Park on 12 March 1952.

The Waggon and Horses Inn. Described as 'a little old fashioned low-roofed roadside inn', it was built about 1700 and demolished about 1870.

The Waggon and Horses Inn. It was situated on the Soho Road approximately where the library is now. Being so close to the Soho Manufactory, there are stories of ' industrial spies' using the Waggon and Horses as their base while they tried to find out more about the latest inventions at Soho.

The Bell Hotel, No. 60 Lozells Road, around 1900. The proprietor was G.A. Asbury.

Woodman Inn on the Holyhead Road on the West Bromwich border by the Hawthorn's football ground, 1900.

Woodman Inn.

The front view of the New Inns in 1901. This building replaced the original inn of the same name which had been on the opposite side of the Holyhead Road. It was constructed in 1798.

The New Inns looking down Sandwell Road. The original inn dated from 1638. It was originally a private house which occasionally opened its doors to stranded travellers.

The back view of the New Inns. The inn was always a prominent feature in the life of Handsworth being the venue for meetings, dinner balls and business lunches. It has now closed as a pub and its grounds have been built over.

The New Inns in November 1901.

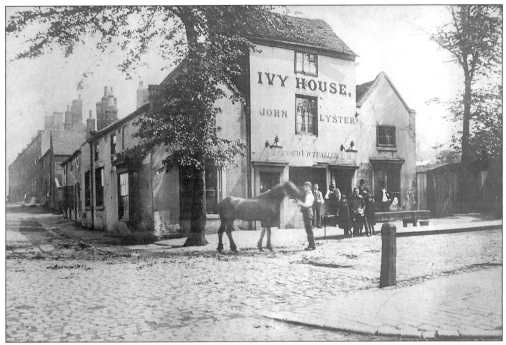

The Old Ivy House Hotel, No. 50 Soho Road, at the corner of Whitehall Road.

The 'New' Ivy House Hotel in 1907. It is now the Gateway To India pub.

The Red Lion inn on Soho Road. Originally a coaching house, its first license was granted in 1542. During the Civil War, Cromwell used the inn for stabling his horses.

The Red Lion, 1906. This inn was built on the same site, in 1902, after the Holt Brewery Company bought up the old inn.

Villa Cross Inn at the corner of Villa and Heathfield Roads. At one time the inn was used as a school for the sons of gentlemen.

The inn, photographed by Thomas Lewis, around 1890. Villa Road can be seen still presenting a very tranquil appearance so different from the bustle and traffic of today.

The Lamp Inn, No. 300 Church Hill, Handsworth Wood, February 1937. Situated opposite Handsworth old church, the Lamp Tavern was described in a sale bill in 1819 as 'most desirably situated for business.' The original building seems to have been added to and given a new frontage in the 1870s. The inn closed in 1937 when the Endwood public house opened next door.

The Leopard Inn, Hockley, in 1901. It was situated at Nos 16 and 17, Great Hampton Street.

Uplands Inn on the Oxhill Road which opened on 16 September 1932.

The Phoenix Tavern, No. 259 Wattville Road, built in 1938. The licensee then was Harvey Blount.

A postcard of Villa Cross picture house. The cinema in Heathfield Road opened as the New Picture House in 1915. It showed Indian films in the 1970s and later became a bingo hall.

The imposing Regal cinema, a landmark at the top end of Soho Road, at its opening in 1929. It was Birmingham's largest suburban cinema seating 2,150 cinemagoers. In later years it was known as the Handsworth ABC before the final curtain came down in 1968.

The New Palladium cinema, Soho Hill, Hockley, 1927. This was a rebuilt and enlarged replacement of the Hockley picture house which originally opened in 1911. It finally closed as a cinema in 1965.

The Elite cinema on the Soho Road, photographed in 1984 when it was an Indian cinema. It had opened in September 1913.

Handsworth (Victoria) Park extension, midsummer 1896. This is the view facing the railway embankment. The brook on the left ran on to Hamstead Road. The boys were the sons of the photographer, Phillip Whitehouse, the chairman of the Handsworth Photographic Society.

A view of the same brook looking towards Hamstead Road taken at Christmas 1895.

Handsworth Park extension in Grove Lane. This photograph was taken from the old boundary of the park towards what was Kemp's farm. The expanded park was formally declared open 'to the people for ever' by the Earl of Dartmouth on 30 March 1898.

Further land taken to extend the park. The extensions more than trebled the size of the park from the original 21 acres up to 69 acres.

HANDSWORTH PARK & CHURCH.

The park and the adjoining Handsworth old church. The growing suburbanization of the district in the 1870s greatly reduced the open land accessible to Handsworth's inhabitants and, despite the opposition of some local taxpayers, the local council agreed to the purchase of land to build a park. The park, called Victoria Park, opened to the public in 1888.

A drinking fountain in the park.

Two views of the fountain. Presented to the park by Austin Lines JP in 1888, the octagonal iron 'umbrello', to give it its proper name, is a Grade II listed building.

Two photographs of the boating pool separated by, probably half a century, but each conveying the same peaceful atmosphere.

A restful corner of the park, photographed in August 1952. In 1911 the park passed into the care of Birmingham Corporation in the shape of the City's Parks Committee, with a staff of over sixteen to maintain its splendour.

The entrance to the park from Hinstock Road, 1956.

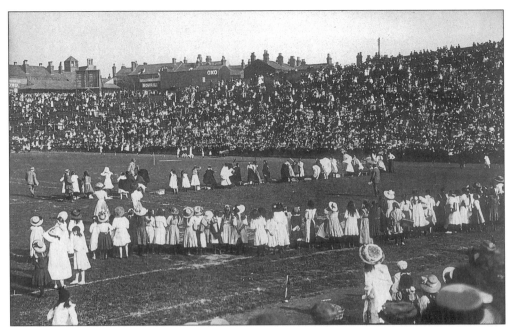

A display of girl's sports. The park has been the venue for a host of events including flower and dog shows, scout rallies and carnivals.

Tennis coaching with Mr Cross. There have been all sorts of sports facilities in the park over the years including cricket, tennis, bowls and putting.

Sons of Rest Pavilion. Handsworth Park was the first park in the city to formally open a council run shelter specifically for the use of local aged men, after complaints that the shelter they normally used let in the rain. The pavilion was opened in February 1930.

Playing billiards in the pavilion in 1952. These shelters were very popular up to a few years ago, but they have now all disappeared from Birmingham's parks.

Park House situated in Grove Lane. This large white house was first known as 'The Grove' until it was bought by Handsworth UDC and used for park purposes from 1887.

Bowling Green, Handsworth Park.

Park House and the bowling green. The house was pulled down in 1968.

Eight
Scenes in Handsworth and Hockley

Old cottages which stood by the Brook where Factory Road joins Piers Road, May 1907.

The shops at Nos 193 to 201, Soho Road, in 1870.

The same shops in 1901. According to the local directory they included a fruiterer, printer, ironmonger and boot manufacturer.

Hockley Hill, The High Pavement, 1900.

The Low Level Pavement, Soho Hill near Hockley Brook, around 1890. It was demolished shortly after this photograph was taken.

Francis Egington's workshop, Prospect House, Soho Hill, 1871. Egington, originally from Bilston, was a designer of stained glass windows of which there are examples in Lichfield and Salisbury Cathedrals. He worked at the Soho Manufactory and was a member of the Lunar Society before he left to set up his own workshop in 1784.

An old cottage, Soho Hill, at one time occupied by one of Matthew Boulton's gamekeepers.

The corner of Villa Road and Soho Road, 1909.

Lambert's, the greengrocers, No. 129 Villa Road, around 1896.

Soho Road junction with Boulton Road in the 1950s.

A confectioner's shop, No. 261a Soho Road.

Soho Road, June 1958.

Soho Road shops, looking towards the city. The council house and library are in the far right of the picture.

The construction of Hockley flyover. A Public Works Department photograph taken in April 1966. The flyover greatly reduced congestion at a notorious traffic bottle neck where the inner circle route crossed the Soho Hill.

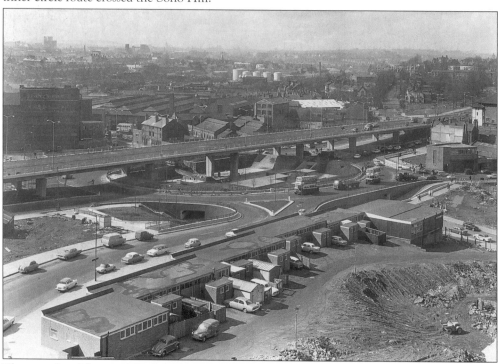

The completed flyover, March 1968.

Old houses in Factory Road, with the Hockley Brook in the foreground, June 1897.

The only surviving photograph in the library's collection of tenement housing in Handsworth and Hockley. This was Court One at the top of Nineveh Road, 1901.

The old coalyard kept by Mr Brown just inside Crove Lane, around 1907.

The old toll gate at the junction of Villa and Hamstead Roads. In 1727, the first toll gates appeared in Handsworth. The gate was removed in 1872. For many years afterwards the house was used as a private school for girls.

A view of Slade Lane which was a narrow byway from Nineveh Road to Piers Road, around 1890.

The site used for bull baiting in Handsworth. The 'sport' was allegedly watched by spectators from the tree in the photograph. As late as 1829, a bull bait was recorded as taking place here. It was said that coaches were delayed deliberately at the end of Queens Head Lane to watch the baiting.

Island Road, Handsworth, 1925.

Bomb damage in Rookery Road, 13 August 1942.

More bomb damage, this time to the rear of Douglas Road, 14 January 1941.

Rowberry's Garage, No. 264 Oxhill Road.

Green's the grocery shop, No. 164 Oxhill Road, at the corner of Friary Road.

Taylor's the greengrocers, No. 308, on Rookery Road junction.

Claremont Road off Soho Hill, February 1963.

Nine
Scenes in Handsworth Wood

Church Lane, 1937. Church Lane was originally a bridle path leading to St Mary's church and was also known as Field Lane.

The junction of Church Lane and Hamstead Road, 1896.

Church Lane, September 1931.

Old cottages in Church Lane, sadly demolished in the late 1950s. They dated back to 1699 and were lovely reminders of Handsworth's rural past.

The cottages in 1933.

Wood Lane, 1934.

Wood Lane, 1934. It was
presumably named because it ran
through part of the wood nearby.

Hamstead Hall Road in 1934.

Calthorpe Cottages in Wood Lane, 1934. They were used in the eighteenth century as estate cottages but were probably built a century before. They have now been converted into four cottages and are Grade II listed buildings.

Brown's Green Lodge, 1933. This was the lodge to the eighteenth-century Brown's Green House situated at the back of what is now a triangle with Handsworth Wood Road and Englestede Close. The house itself was demolished at the end of the last century after becoming the original Hamstead Hill school. The lodge is a Grade II listed building.

Brown's Green, 1934.

Brown's Green, 1934. This was one of several 'Greens' in Handsworth. The first mention of it was in 1535, when it was described as a croft owned by Roger Browne at a yearly rental of 5s.

Hamstead Road, 1923. From the postcard series 'Souvenirs of Handsworth'.

A more recent postcard view of Hamstead Road.

The old school gatehouse, Handsworth Wood Road, in 1937. Handsworth Wood Road is one of Handsworth's oldest roads. It was turnpiked in 1787.

The lodge to the friary in the late 1890s. There were two lodges to the house, this one was opposite the corner of Friary and College Roads. (See the friary on p. 52)

The two lodges to the friary.

The lodge and avenue to Oxhill House, 1898. There were two lodges to this delightfully situated old house, now gone; one was in Sandwell Road and the other in Rookery Road. One of the attractions of the house was its extensive views of the surrounding countryside.

A view in Heathfield Road taken from Mayfield Road. The Baptist chapel is in the background.

Two views of Handsworth Wood railway station. The station was opened by the London and North Western Railway Company on 1 January 1896 and closed by the London, Midland and Scottish Company on 5 May 1941. In its heyday it would have had an extensive staff some of whom are pictured in the top photograph. The line on the Soho Loop was laid to allow freight trains to bypass New Street station.